How To Make $1 Million With Bitcoin

By Thomas Spiteri

Chapters

1. Introduction to Bitcoin: The Basics of Blockchain Technology and Cryptocurrency
2. Understanding the Bitcoin Economy: Market Analysis and Investment Strategies
3. Bitcoin Mining: The Process of Creating New Bitcoins
4. Bitcoin Transactions and Wallet Management: How to Buy, Sell, and Secure Your Bitcoins
5. The Legal and Regulatory Landscape of Bitcoin: Navigating the Complex World of Cryptocurrency Laws
6. Bitcoin and the Future of Payment Systems: How Blockchain Technology is Changing the Way We Pay for Goods and Services
7. Bitcoin and Blockchain for Business: How Companies are Using the Technology to Disrupt Industries
8. Advanced Topics in Bitcoin: From Smart Contracts to Lightning Networks
9. Bitcoin Security and Privacy: Protecting Your Digital Assets from Hackers and Scammers
10. Conclusion: The Impact of Bitcoin on the Global Financial System and the Future of Money.
11. Bonus Chapter: the best companies to buy manage and secure your bitcoins.

Chapter 1
The Basics of Blockchain Technology and Cryptocurrency

In this first chapter we will provide an overview of the history, technology, and current state of the cryptocurrency known as Bitcoin. This chapter will cover the origins of Bitcoin, its underlying blockchain technology, and its current use cases. We will also discuss the key concepts and terms related to Bitcoin, such as mining, wallets, and smart contracts. By the end of this chapter, readers will have a solid understanding of the basics of Bitcoin and the potential impact it may have on the future of finance and technology

1. The origin of Bitcoin:

The origins of Bitcoin can be traced back to the 2008 white paper written by the pseudonymous Satoshi Nakamoto. This paper, entitled "Bitcoin: A Peer-to-Peer Electronic Cash System," described a new type of decentralized digital currency that could be transferred directly between individuals without the need for a central authority. The key innovation behind Bitcoin was the use of a blockchain, a distributed ledger that records every transaction and is maintained by a network of computers. This technology ensured that all transactions were transparent, secure, and tamper-proof, and it paved the way for the development of other cryptocurrencies

2. Blockchain Technology

Blockchain technology is the backbone of the cryptocurrency, Bitcoin, and is essentially a digital ledger that records and verifies transactions across a decentralized network of computers. It is a decentralized and distributed ledger that records all transactions in a secure and transparent manner. The technology uses cryptography to secure the transactions and to control the creation of new units of a particular cryptocurrency. Each block in the chain contains a number of transactions and a reference to the previous block, creating a chain of blocks, hence the name blockchain. This allows the network to maintain a consistent and unchangeable record of all transactions without the need for a centralized intermediary.

3. Current use

Bitcoin has been used for a variety of purposes since its creation, including as a store of value, a medium of exchange, and a speculative investment. One of the most well-known use cases for Bitcoin is as a form of digital gold, as it shares many of the same characteristics as gold, including scarcity and decentralization. Additionally, Bitcoin has been used as a means of payment for goods and services, particularly in the online space where traditional payment methods may not be as easily accessible. More recently, Bitcoin has also been used as a speculative investment, with many buying and holding the cryptocurrency with the expectation of its value increasing over time. The use of Bitcoin has also been used to facilitate illegal activities, such as money laundering, because of its ability to move funds quickly and anonymously.

4. Mining

Mining is the process by which new bitcoin transactions are added to the blockchain, the public ledger of all bitcoin transactions. It is also the process by which new bitcoins are created. The process of mining involves using specialized software to solve complex mathematical problems that are used to validate and record transactions on the blockchain. As a reward for their efforts, miners are given a certain amount of new bitcoins. The process of mining is designed to be resource-intensive, so it requires a significant amount of computational power. This is to ensure that creating new bitcoins is a costly process and that the supply of bitcoin is limited, as outlined in the original white paper.

5. Wallets

A Bitcoin wallet is a software program where Bitcoins are stored. To be technically accurate, Bitcoins are not stored anywhere; there is a private key (secret number) for every Bitcoin address that is saved in the Bitcoin wallet of the person who owns the balance. Bitcoin wallets facilitate sending and receiving Bitcoins and give ownership of the Bitcoin balance to the user. The Bitcoin wallet comes in many forms; desktop, mobile, web, and hardware are the four main types of wallets

6. Smart Contracts

Smart contracts are self-executing contracts with the terms of the agreement between buyer and seller being directly written into lines of code. The code and the agreements it enforces exist over a decentralized network and execute automatically. Smart contracts allow for the automation of digital assets and enable the creation of decentralized apps (dApps) on blockchain networks. They have the potential to streamline and automate many industries, from real estate to supply chain management.

Chapter 2
Understanding the Bitcoin Economy: Market Analysis and Investment Strategies

In this chapter, we will delve into the current state of the Bitcoin market and explore different strategies for analyzing and investing in Bitcoin. We will start by discussing the basics of market analysis, including technical analysis, fundamental analysis, and sentiment analysis.

Next, we will explore the different investment strategies, such as holding, trading, and mining, and the pros and cons of each. We will also cover the concept of diversification and how to create a well-rounded portfolio of cryptocurrencies.

Additionally, we will discuss the risks and benefits of investing in Bitcoin and how to protect yourself against potential losses. By the end of this chapter, you will have a solid understanding of the Bitcoin market and how to create a profitable investment strategy.

1. **The Bitcoin market**

As of to date, almost 19 million have been mined out of the 21 million supplies
Basically only 2 million left to be mined, so you can expect the price of bitcoin to go up exponentially.

The next bitcoin halving is due to be around May 2024.

What is halving and how does it affect the mining of Bitcoin?

A bitcoin halving (sometimes 'halvening') is an event where the reward for mining new blocks is halved, meaning miners receive 50% fewer bitcoins for verifying transactions. Bitcoin halvings are scheduled to occur once every 210,000 blocks – roughly every four years – until the maximum supply of 21 million bitcoins has been generated by the network.

Bitcoin halvings are important events for traders because they reduce the number of new bitcoins being generated by the network. This limits the supply of new coins, so prices could rise if demand remains strong. While this has happened in the months before and after previous halvings – causing bitcoin's price to appreciate rapidly – the circumstances surrounding each halving are different and demand for bitcoin can fluctuate wildly.

2. The different strategies for analysing and investing in Bitcoin

Holding remains the best strategy to invest in Bitcoin. Bitcoin will hit $1 million per coin within a 15-to-20-year range. Although it has been very volatile and will remain volatile, Bitcoin has been following the Nasdaq like any other securities, so it is fair to say that it has own its place as a digital store of value, a digital gold in essence.

Trading bitcoin can be rewarding if you know exactly what you are doing and have the technical knowledge to do so. Those who are trading on margin are taking risk especially in the uncertain times we are now.

A flash crash and you are facing a margin call and risk losing all your investments and we saw it time and time again.
But if you look where Bitcoin was in 2015 and now, then you see that you are in the money if you had invested at the right time.

Is it too late to invest? Absolutely not and you should consider recurring buying with whatever you can save. But bitcoin should not constitute 100% of your portfolio.

If you are a trader with some technical knowledge, then you can use the Moving Average and Relative Strength Index (RSI) as well as other technical charts to determine Buy and Sell signals.

Is mining a viable option?

Mining on your own is costly but some companies are offering Mining services such as
FEEL MINING (www.feel-mining.com)
They are a regulated company by the AMF which is the French equivalent of the SEC.

Do not subscribe to mining companies that are not regulated or you will risk losing your investment.

Mining Bitcoin or ETH should be a long-term investment strategy and there is cost associated with it.
There are a lot of crypto currencies available on the market but only a few have real projects associated with it. So do not be fool in buying cheap coins, usually called shitty coins
Anyone can create a token but 99.99% of the time, they are not back up by any projects whatsoever.

Bitcoin and Ethereum are essentially the only crypto you should really invest in for the long term.

Chapter 3
Bitcoin Mining: The Process of Creating New Bitcoins

1. The technical aspects of Bitcoin mining, including the use of specialized hardware and software, and the process of solving complex mathematical problems to validate transactions and create new bitcoins.

2. The economics of Bitcoin mining, including the costs of electricity, hardware, and other expenses, and the potential returns on investment for miners.

3. The different types of mining pools, their pros and cons, and how to choose the best one for your needs.

4. The future of Bitcoin mining, including the potential impact of advances in technology and changes in the regulatory environment.

5. How to set up and operate a profitable Bitcoin mining operation, including tips on how to minimize costs and maximize returns.

6. Case studies of successful Bitcoin mining operations, and lessons learned from the experiences of experienced miners.

1. **The technical aspects of Bitcoin mining**:

Bitcoin mining is the process by which new bitcoins are created. It is a decentralized process that is done by a network of computers solving complex mathematical equations. The process is designed to be difficult, so that only a specific number of new bitcoins can be created each day. The exact number of new bitcoins created per day is determined by a mathematical formula called the "block reward," which is designed to decrease over time. This is done to control the total supply of bitcoins and to keep the value of the currency stable.

The technical aspects of Bitcoin mining involve using specialized software to solve complex mathematical equations. These equations are part of the process that confirms transactions on the Bitcoin network. When a miner solves one of these equations, they are rewarded with a certain number of new bitcoins. The process of mining also helps to secure the Bitcoin network by confirming transactions and making it difficult for any one person or group to control the network.

To mine Bitcoin, you need a computer with a powerful graphics processing unit (GPU) and specialized mining software. You also need access to a large amount of electricity, as the process of mining can be quite power-intensive. The difficulty of mining Bitcoin has increased significantly over time, and today it is typically only profitable for those who have access to large amounts of computational power and cheap electricity.

2. The economics of Bitcoin Mining:

The economics of Bitcoin mining are complex and can be affected by a variety of factors, including the cost of electricity, the cost of hardware, and other expenses.

One of the main costs associated with Bitcoin mining is the cost of electricity. Miners need to run their powerful computers 24/7 in order to keep up with the competition and maintain their position in the network. This requires a significant amount of energy, which can be quite costly. In addition to electricity costs, miners also need to invest in specialized hardware, such as ASICs, which can be quite expensive. These costs can add up quickly and eat into any potential returns on investment.

Despite these costs, many miners choose to participate in the Bitcoin network because of the potential rewards. When a miner successfully solves a complex mathematical problem and adds a block to the blockchain, they are rewarded with a certain number of bitcoins. The number of bitcoins rewarded for each block decreases over time, but the value of bitcoins can also increase, making it a potentially profitable endeavor. Additionally, miners may also earn transaction fees for verifying transactions on the blockchain, which can also contribute to their returns on investment.

However, due to the high competition in the mining industry, it can be difficult to predict the potential returns on investment. The cost of hardware and electricity can also change rapidly, making it difficult to estimate the profitability of Bitcoin mining. Additionally, the price of Bitcoin is highly volatile, which can also make it difficult to predict the potential returns on investment. Despite these challenges, many people still choose to mine Bitcoin because of the potential rewards and the opportunity to be a part of a decentralized network that is changing the world of finance.

3. The different types of mining pools, their pros and cons, and how to choose the best one for your needs

Mining pools are groups of miners who combine their computational resources to increase their chances of finding new blocks and earning block rewards. There are several different types of mining pools, each with their own advantages and disadvantages. Some mining pools are large and well-established, while others are small and more experimental.

When choosing a mining pool, it's important to consider factors such as the pool's size, fees, and reward structure. Larger pools may have more consistent payouts, but they may also have higher fees.

On the other hand, smaller pools may have lower fees, but their payouts may be less consistent. Additionally, it's also important to consider the pool's reward structure, as some pools use a proportional system where miners are rewarded based on the amount of computational power they contribute, while others use a pay-per-share system where miners are rewarded based on the number of shares they contribute. Ultimately, the choice of a mining pool will depend on the miner's individual preferences and goals.

One of the most common types of mining pools is the traditional pool, in which miners are paid a fixed reward for each block they help to mine. These pools typically have a low minimum payout threshold and offer steady, consistent payouts.

Another type of mining pool is the pay-per-share (PPS) pool, in which miners are paid based on the number of shares they contribute to the pool. These pools typically have a higher minimum payout threshold, but offer higher payouts per share.

A third type of mining pool is the proportional pool, in which miners are paid based on the proportion of total computational power they contribute to the pool. These pools offer a more variable payout structure, but can be more profitable for miners with powerful hardware.

There are other different types of mining pools such as solo mining pool, PPLNS, PPS+ and more. Each one has its own advantages and disadvantages and it's important to consider them in order to choose the best one for your needs.

4. **The future of Bitcoin mining, including the potential impact of advances in technology and changes in the regulatory environment.**

The future of bitcoin mining is uncertain, it is likely that the mining process will continue to evolve, as advances in technology and changes in the regulatory environment. For example, the increasing use of renewable energy sources and the development of more energy-efficient mining hardware could help to reduce the environmental impact of mining.

Advances in technology are likely to have a significant impact on the future of Bitcoin mining. One of the most important factors is the development of more efficient mining hardware. As hardware becomes more powerful and energy-efficient, the cost of mining Bitcoin will decrease. This could make it more profitable for individuals and small mining operations to participate in the network, potentially decentralizing the mining process.

Another important technological development is the use of specialized chips called Application Specific Integrated Circuits (ASICs) specifically built for the purpose of mining Bitcoin. These chips have increased the efficiency and speed of mining, making it more difficult for individuals to compete with large mining operations.

Additionally, the development of new consensus algorithms such as Proof of Stake (PoS) which is an alternative to the current Proof of Work (PoW) algorithm may change the way the network is secured and how new bitcoins are minted. These new algorithms may also make mining more energy-efficient and less reliant on specialized hardware.

Finally, the regulatory environment is also likely to play a role in the future of Bitcoin mining. Governments around the world are still figuring out how to regulate cryptocurrencies, and changes in regulations could have a big impact on the mining industry. For example, if electricity costs increase due to regulations, it could make mining less profitable and could lead to the centralization of mining operations in regions with more favorable regulations.

5. **How to set up and operate a profitable Bitcoin mining operation, including tips on how to minimize costs and maximize returns.**

In order to set up and operate a profitable Bitcoin mining operation, there are several important factors to consider. The first is the cost of electricity, as this can have a major impact on the overall profitability of the operation. Miners need to find a location with low electricity rates and a reliable source of power.

Another important factor to consider is the cost of hardware. Bitcoin mining requires specialized equipment, such as ASICs (Application-Specific Integrated Circuits), which can be expensive to purchase and maintain. Miners also need to budget for the cost of cooling equipment, as the mining process generates a significant amount of heat.

Miners also need to consider the potential returns on investment. The price of Bitcoin and the difficulty of mining can fluctuate, so it's important to do market analysis and make an informed decision about when to start mining and when to sell mined coins.

Lastly, miners also need to consider the regulations in the countries they operate in, as laws and regulations can greatly impact the profitability of a mining operation. It's important to be aware of any taxes and regulations that apply to mining operations and to stay compliant with them.

When setting up and operating a Bitcoin mining operation, there are a few key strategies that you can use to minimize costs and maximize returns. One important strategy is to carefully choose your mining hardware. This means selecting equipment that is energy-efficient, powerful, and reliable. It's also important to choose a good location for your mining operation, since electricity costs can vary significantly depending on where you are located.

Another important strategy is to join a mining pool. By joining a mining pool, you can share the costs and rewards of mining with other miners, which can help to increase your chances of earning a profit. When choosing a mining pool, it's important to consider the pool's fees, payout structure, and overall reputation.

A cost-saving strategy is to use renewable energy for mining, This can help to significantly reduce the cost of electricity, which is one of the biggest expenses associated with Bitcoin mining. This can be done by setting up your mining operation in a location where renewable energy sources such as solar or hydro power are readily available or by investing in renewable energy equipment like solar panels or wind turbines.

Finally, it's important to stay informed about the latest developments in the Bitcoin mining industry. This includes staying up-to-date on new mining hardware and software, as well as changes in regulations and market conditions. By staying informed, you can make better decisions about how to operate your mining operation, and you can be better prepared to adapt to new challenges as they arise.

Regenerate response

6. **Case studies of successful Bitcoin mining operations, and lessons learned from the experiences of experienced miners.**

1. Location is key. Miners need to find a location with low electricity costs, as energy consumption is the main expense for a mining operation. Some miners have found success in using renewable energy sources such as hydroelectric or geothermal power.
2. Scalability is important. A mining operation should be able to easily expand and upgrade as the mining difficulty increases and new technologies become available.
3. Networking is crucial. Joining a mining pool or creating a mining consortium can help miners increase their chances of finding new blocks and earning rewards.

4. Stay informed. Keeping up to date with the latest developments in the Bitcoin mining industry and regulatory changes can help miners make better decisions and stay competitive.
5. Look at the big picture. Bitcoin mining is a long-term investment, and miners should have a clear understanding of the potential risks and rewards before diving in.
6. Diversify your mining operation. Some experienced miners have diversified their mining operations by mining other cryptocurrencies in addition to Bitcoin. This can help to offset the risk of mining one specific cryptocurrency.

Some of the most reputable bitcoin mining companies are:

1. Marathon Digital Holdings (MARA)

Marathon Digital Holdings, Inc. is a digital asset technology company, which engages in mining cryptocurrencies with a focus on the blockchain ecosystem and the generation of digital assets. The company was founded on February 23, 2010 and is headquartered in Las Vegas, NV.

2. RIOT Platforms Inc (RIOT)

Riot Platforms, Inc. is a bitcoin mining company engaged in the provision of special cryptocurrency mining computers. It invests in Verady, Coinsquare, and Tess. The company was founded on July 24, 2000 and is headquartered in Castle Rock, CO.

Their share price is dependent of the Bitcoin price but at the same time investing in the underlying value of Bitcoin through mining companies is a smart investment and must be considered for the long term as part of a diverse portfolio.

Chapter 4
Bitcoin Transactions and Wallet Management: How to Buy, Sell, and Secure Your Bitcoins

When it comes to buying and selling Bitcoins, there are a variety of methods you can use. One popular way is to use a cryptocurrency exchange, such as Coinbase or Binance, which allows you to buy and sell Bitcoins (and other cryptocurrencies) using fiat currency (e.g. USD, EUR) or other cryptocurrencies.

Another option is to use a peer-to-peer marketplace, such as LocalBitcoins, www.bitcoin.de, which connects buyers and sellers directly. In this case, you may be able to purchase Bitcoins using cash or a bank transfer, depending on the seller's preferences.

Once you have obtained some Bitcoins, it's important to store them securely. One way to do this is to use a software wallet, such as the Bitcoin Core wallet or Mycelium, which allows you to control your own private keys. Another option is to use a hardware wallet, such as a Trezor or Ledger, which stores your private keys on a secure device that is separate from your computer.

It's also essential to keep your computer and mobile device safe from malware and viruses, and to use a strong and unique password for your wallet. Keep your recovery seed in a safe place and avoid sharing your private key with anyone. Additionally, make sure that you are buying from a reputable seller, and do your own research about the company you are buying from before making your purchase.

Coinbase is probably the best company in the US and bitcoin.de in the EU to buy your Bitcoins. Both companies are regulated in their respective country and do not operate offshore.

You can set up a recurring buy on Coinbase making it easier to save for the long term.

Coinbase has over 150 crypto currencies listed there so it is easier to diversify your portfolio. But again make sure you do your research before buying as not all of them are backed up by a serious and reliable project.

Chapter 5
The Legal and Regulatory Landscape of Bitcoin:
Navigating the Complex World of Cryptocurrency Laws

1. An overview of the current legal status of Bitcoin and other cryptocurrencies in different countries around the world.
2. The regulatory frameworks that have been put in place by governments to oversee the use and trading of cryptocurrencies, such as the requirement for exchanges to register with financial authorities and implement know-your-customer (KYC) and anti-money laundering (AML) measures.
3. The potential legal risks and challenges faced by businesses and individuals who use Bitcoin, such as issues related to taxation, securities laws, and money transmission regulations.
4. The ongoing debate over how best to regulate and legislate for the use of Bitcoin and other cryptocurrencies, and the different approaches being taken by governments and international organizations.
5. How to navigate the legal and regulatory landscape of Bitcoin and other cryptocurrencies, including tips on compliance and best practices for businesses and individuals.
6. The future of cryptocurrency regulations
7. The potential impact of regulations on the growth and adoption of Bitcoin and other cryptocurrencies

1. An overview of the current legal status of Bitcoin and other cryptocurrencies in different countries around the world.

The legal status of Bitcoin and other cryptocurrencies varies greatly from country to country. In some countries, such as Japan and South Korea, Bitcoin and other cryptocurrencies are fully legal and regulated, and can be bought, sold, and used for transactions just like any other currency. In other countries, such as China and Russia, the use of Bitcoin and other cryptocurrencies is heavily restricted or outright banned.

In the United States, the legal status of Bitcoin and other cryptocurrencies is still somewhat unclear. The IRS has classified Bitcoin as property for tax purposes, but the SEC and other regulatory agencies are still working to develop a comprehensive framework for regulating the use of cryptocurrencies. This has led to a patchwork of state-level regulations and guidelines, which can make it difficult for individuals and businesses to navigate the legal landscape of Bitcoin and other cryptocurrencies.

In general, it is important for individuals and businesses to stay informed about the legal and regulatory developments related to Bitcoin and other cryptocurrencies in their country, as well as any international laws that may apply. It is also important to seek professional legal advice when engaging in any transactions or activities related to Bitcoin or other cryptocurrencies.

In terms of regulation, some countries have regulatory sandbox for crypto-assets, which is a regulatory framework that allows innovators to test new crypto-asset related products, services or business models in a live environment under the watchful eye of the regulator. This is being done to have a better understanding of the crypto-assets and blockchain technology, and to provide regulatory clarity to the industry participants.

That said here are the most friendly- Bitcoin countries in the world to date.

- Switzerland.
- Luxembourg.
- Gibraltar.
- El Salvador.
- Singapore.
- Estonia.

- Germany.
- Portugal.

Crypto Tax-Free Countries:

- Cayman Islands. Tax Residency.
- El Salvador. Tax Residency.
- Germany. Tax Residency.
- Malaysia. Tax Residency.
- Malta. Tax Residency.
- Portugal. Tax Residency.

2. **The regulatory frameworks that have been put in place by governments to oversee the use and trading of cryptocurrencies, such as the requirement for exchanges to register with financial authorities and implement know-your-customer (KYC) and anti-money laundering (AML) measures.**

The legal and regulatory landscape of Bitcoin and other cryptocurrencies varies greatly from country to country. In some countries, such as Japan and South Korea, Bitcoin and other cryptocurrencies are fully legal and regulated, with exchanges required to register with financial authorities and implement know-your-customer (KYC) and anti-money laundering (AML) measures. In other countries, such as China and India, the use of cryptocurrencies is heavily restricted or outright banned.

To navigate the complex world of cryptocurrency laws, it is important to stay up to date on the latest developments and regulatory frameworks in different countries. This can include monitoring official government announcements and guidance, as well as keeping tabs on the actions of regulatory bodies such as the Securities and Exchange Commission (SEC) in the United States and the Financial Conduct Authority (FCA) in the United Kingdom.

It's also important to be aware that laws and regulations can change rapidly, so it's important to stay informed and adapt to new rules and requirements as they come out. Additionally, some countries may have different laws and regulations for different types of cryptocurrencies, so it's important to understand the specific rules that apply to the cryptocurrency you're interested in.

Additionally, it's also important to consider the tax implications of buying, selling, and holding Bitcoin and other cryptocurrencies. In many countries, cryptocurrency transactions are subject to capital gains taxes, and it's important to be aware of these tax obligations and to keep accurate records of your transactions.

Considering that laws are always changing and sometime not in your favour, choosing the right jurisdiction for your investment is key and critical.

If you hold a lot of Bitcoins, then it would make sense to move to a tax friendly country.

3. The potential legal risks and challenges faced by businesses and individuals who use Bitcoin, such as issues related to taxation, securities laws, and money transmission regulations

The potential legal risks and challenges faced by businesses and individuals who use Bitcoin can vary depending on the country or jurisdiction in which they operate. Some of the key issues to consider include:

- Taxation: Bitcoin and other cryptocurrencies are often treated as property for tax purposes, which means that they may be subject to capital gains taxes when they are sold or exchanged for other currencies. However, the tax treatment of Bitcoin can vary widely from country to country, and it is important to be aware of the specific rules and regulations in your jurisdiction.

- Securities laws: Depending on how Bitcoin is used and marketed, it may be considered a security and therefore subject to securities laws. This can be especially relevant for initial coin offerings (ICOs) and other fundraising mechanisms that involve the sale of tokens or other digital assets.

- Money transmission regulations: Bitcoin and other cryptocurrencies are often considered a form of money or value, and as such, they may be subject to regulations that govern the transmission of funds. This can include requirements for licensing, registration, and compliance with anti-money laundering (AML) and know-your-customer (KYC) regulations.

Overall, it is important to be aware of the legal and regulatory landscape of Bitcoin and other cryptocurrencies, and to seek professional advice if you have any questions or concerns about how these laws may apply to your specific situation.

4. **The ongoing debate over how best to regulate and legislate for the use of Bitcoin and other cryptocurrencies, and the different approaches being taken by governments and international organizations.**

The ongoing debate over how best to regulate and legislate for the use of Bitcoin and other cryptocurrencies is a complex and multifaceted issue. On one hand, there are those who argue that cryptocurrencies should be treated as traditional financial assets and subject to the same regulations as other forms of money. This would involve implementing regulations to prevent money laundering and other illegal activities, as well as measures to protect consumers and investors.

On the other hand, there are those who argue that cryptocurrencies should be treated differently from traditional financial assets, due to their decentralized nature and the potential for them to be used for innovative and disruptive purposes. This would involve taking a more hands-off approach to regulation, allowing the technology to develop and evolve without stifling innovation.

Governments and international organizations are taking different approaches to the regulation of cryptocurrencies. Some countries, such as Japan and South Korea, have embraced the technology and have put in place regulations to encourage its development and use. Other countries, such as China and India, have taken a more cautious approach, implementing strict regulations to limit the use of cryptocurrencies.

The regulatory environment for cryptocurrencies is constantly changing, as governments and international organizations continue to grapple with how best to regulate this new and rapidly evolving technology. It is important for businesses and individuals who use Bitcoin to stay informed about the legal and regulatory landscape in their respective countries, and to consult with legal experts to ensure that they are in compliance with all applicable laws and regulations.

5. How to navigate the legal and regulatory landscape of Bitcoin and other cryptocurrencies, including tips on compliance and best practices for businesses and individuals.

Navigating the legal and regulatory landscape of Bitcoin and other cryptocurrencies can be complex, as the laws and regulations vary from country to country and are still evolving in many places. Here are a few tips on how to navigate this landscape:

1. Research the laws and regulations in your country or region: Understand the current legal status of Bitcoin and other cryptocurrencies in your country, as well as any laws and regulations that apply to their use and trading.
2. Stay up to date on changes and developments: The laws and regulations regarding cryptocurrencies are constantly evolving, so it's important to stay informed about any changes or new developments.
3. Understand the requirements for compliance: Many countries require businesses and individuals who use Bitcoin and other cryptocurrencies to comply with certain laws and regulations, such as know-your-customer (KYC) and anti-money laundering (AML) measures. Make sure you understand these requirements and take steps to comply with them.
4. Seek professional advice: If you are a business or individual that uses or plans to use Bitcoin or other cryptocurrencies, it's a good idea to consult with a legal professional or accountant who is familiar with the laws and regulations in your country.
5. Be aware of the possible risks: Using Bitcoin and other cryptocurrencies may involve certain legal risks, such as issues related to taxation, securities laws, and money transmission regulations. Be aware of these risks and take steps to mitigate them.
6. Follow best practices: Adopt best practices for using and managing your Bitcoin and other cryptocurrencies, such as keeping your private keys safe, using a reputable wallet, and only dealing with trusted parties.

6. The future of cryptocurrency regulations

The future of cryptocurrency regulations is uncertain and can vary depending on the country and region. Some countries have been more open to embracing cryptocurrencies and have put in place relatively permissive regulations, while others have outright banned their use.

In general, it's expected that governments will continue to take a closer look at the use and trading of cryptocurrencies and may put in place more stringent regulations in order to address concerns around money laundering, fraud, and other financial crimes. This could include increased oversight of cryptocurrency exchanges, stricter requirements for customer identification and verification, and new rules around taxation.

On the other hand, some experts like Larry Fink CEO of Blackrock believe that the technology behind cryptocurrencies, particularly blockchain, has the potential to revolutionize industries beyond just finance. This could lead to more relaxed regulations and government adoption in the future.

International organizations such as the G20 and the Financial Action Task Force (FATF) have also been discussing potential global standards for cryptocurrency regulation. However, due to the decentralized nature of cryptocurrencies, it is unlikely for a global consensus to be reached easily.

7. The potential impact of regulations on the growth and adoption of Bitcoin and other cryptocurrencies

The potential impact of regulations on the growth and adoption of Bitcoin and other cryptocurrencies is a topic of ongoing debate. On one hand, some argue that regulations can provide greater legitimacy and stability to the market, making it more attractive to businesses and investors. Regulations can also help to prevent illegal activities such as money laundering and fraud. On the other hand, others argue that heavy regulations could stifle innovation and limit the appeal of cryptocurrencies as a decentralized alternative to traditional financial systems.

In terms of specific regulations, there are a number of areas where governments have begun to take action. One of the most significant is the requirement for exchanges to register with financial authorities and implement know-your-customer (KYC) and anti-money laundering (AML) measures. These regulations are intended to prevent illegal activities such as money laundering and fraud, but they can also make it more difficult for individuals to use Bitcoin and other cryptocurrencies anonymously.

Another area of regulatory focus has been taxation. In many countries, Bitcoin and other cryptocurrencies are treated as property for tax purposes, meaning that individuals and businesses must pay taxes on any capital gains when they sell or trade their coins. This can create additional complexity and compliance costs for users and may also discourage some people from using Bitcoin and other cryptocurrencies.

Finally, there are ongoing debates over how to regulate the use of Bitcoin and other cryptocurrencies in areas such as securities laws and money transmission regulations. Some governments have taken a more hands-off approach, while others have proposed or implemented more restrictive measures. As the market continues to evolve, it is likely that the regulatory landscape will continue to change as well. The future of the regulations is uncertain, and it depends on how the market and the governments adapt to the new technology.

Chapter 6
Bitcoin and the Future of Payment Systems: How Blockchain Technology is Changing the Way We Pay for Goods and Services

Blockchain technology, the underlying technology behind Bitcoin and other cryptocurrencies, has the potential to revolutionize the way we pay for goods and services. One of the key benefits of blockchain technology is its ability to enable secure, decentralized, and transparent transactions. This means that transactions can be completed without the need for a central intermediary, such as a bank, and can be tracked and verified by anyone on the blockchain network.

One of the major ways that blockchain technology is changing the way we pay for goods and services is through the use of cryptocurrency. Bitcoin and other cryptocurrencies can be used to make payments for goods and services just like traditional fiat currencies. The advantage of using cryptocurrency is that transactions can be completed faster and at a lower cost than traditional payment methods. Additionally, cryptocurrency transactions are generally more secure, as they are protected by advanced encryption and are not subject to fraud or chargebacks.

Another way blockchain technology is changing the way we pay for goods and services is through the use of smart contracts. Smart contracts are self-executing contracts with the terms of the agreement between buyer and seller being directly written into lines of code. These contracts are stored and replicated on the blockchain network and can be automatically executed when certain conditions are met. Smart contracts can be used to facilitate various types of transactions, including the exchange of money, goods, and services.

Finally, blockchain technology has the potential to change the way we pay for goods and services through the use of decentralized marketplaces and platforms. These platforms can use smart contracts and blockchain technology to enable peer-to-peer transactions without the need for a central intermediary. This can lead to more efficient and cost-effective marketplaces, with lower transaction fees and less fraud.

In summary, blockchain technology has the potential to change the way we pay for goods and services by enabling secure, decentralized, and transparent transactions through the use of cryptocurrency, smart contracts, and decentralized marketplaces.

Chapter 7
Bitcoin and Blockchain for Business: How Companies are Using the Technology to Disrupt Industries

Blockchain technology is a revolutionary new way of storing and sharing data that has the potential to disrupt many different industries. One of the key ways in which it is changing the way we pay for goods and services is through the use of cryptocurrencies like Bitcoin. These digital currencies use blockchain technology to enable fast, secure, and borderless transactions without the need for intermediaries like banks or credit card companies.

Companies in a wide range of industries are starting to explore the potential of blockchain technology and are using it to create new and innovative products and services. For example, in the finance industry, blockchain is being used to create decentralized exchanges and platforms for peer-to-peer lending and crowdfunding. In the supply chain industry, blockchain is being used to create more transparent and efficient systems for tracking the movement of goods and ensuring that they are ethically sourced.

Another area where blockchain is having a significant impact is in the area of digital identity. Blockchain-based systems can be used to create secure, decentralized, and tamper-proof digital identities that can be used for a wide range of purposes, such as voting, banking, and accessing government services.

Finally, blockchain is also being used to create new business models and revenue streams. For example, blockchain-based platforms like Steemit and Akasha are using blockchain to create decentralized social media networks where users are rewarded with cryptocurrency for creating and curating content. And blockchain-based platforms like Ethereum are enabling the creation of decentralized autonomous organizations (DAOs) that can operate without the need for human oversight.

Overall, blockchain technology is changing the way we pay for goods and services and is enabling companies to disrupt traditional industries and create new business models.

Chapter 8
Advanced Topics in Bitcoin: From Smart Contracts to Lightning Networks

The evolution of blockchain technology has led to the development of new features and capabilities beyond the basic concept of a decentralized ledger. One such development is the use of smart contracts, which are self-executing contracts with the terms of the agreement written directly into lines of code. This allows for automatic execution of the contract as soon as certain predefined conditions are met. Smart contracts can be used for a wide range of applications, from supply chain management to real estate transactions.

Another development in blockchain technology is the use of Lightning Networks, which are designed to increase the scalability and speed of transactions on the Bitcoin and other blockchain networks. This is achieved by creating a second layer on top of the blockchain that can handle a high volume of small transactions off-chain, with only the final results being recorded on the blockchain. This can greatly reduce the amount of data that needs to be processed and stored on the blockchain, allowing for faster and cheaper transactions.

The use of smart contracts and lightning networks are just two examples of how blockchain technology is being developed to meet the changing needs of businesses and consumers. As the technology continues to evolve, we can expect to see even more innovative uses and capabilities in the future.

As the technology is evolving, companies and entrepreneurs are finding more and more ways to apply it to various industries. From finance, to healthcare, to logistics, blockchain technology is helping companies to disrupt traditional business models, increase transparency and efficiency, and create new opportunities for growth and innovation.

Chapter 9
Bitcoin Security and Privacy: Protecting Your Digital Assets from Hackers and Scammers

Protecting your digital assets, such as Bitcoin and other cryptocurrencies, from hackers and scammers is a critical aspect of using these assets. Here are a few tips to help you keep your assets safe:

1. Use a hardware wallet: Hardware wallets are physical devices that store your private keys offline, making them much more difficult to hack than software wallets.
2. Enable two-factor authentication: Two-factor authentication (2FA) adds an extra layer of security by requiring a code from your phone in addition to your password.
3. Keep your software updated: Regularly updating your software, including your operating system and any wallet software, can help protect you from known vulnerabilities.
4. Be wary of phishing attempts: Scammers may try to trick you into giving them your private keys or seed phrases by pretending to be a legitimate website or service. Always double-check the URL and be cautious of clicking on links in emails or messages.
5. Avoid public Wi-Fi: Public Wi-Fi networks can be vulnerable to hacking, so it's best to avoid using them to access your digital assets.
6. Educate yourself: Stay informed about the latest scams and hacking attempts so you know what to look out for.
7. Diversify your assets: Instead of keeping all your digital assets in one place, consider spreading them out across different wallets and services to minimize your risk.

By following these guidelines and being vigilant, you can help protect your digital assets from hackers and scammers.

Chapter 10
Conclusion: The Impact of Bitcoin on the Global Financial System and the Future of Money

Bitcoin and other cryptocurrencies have the potential to greatly impact the global financial system and the way we think about money. One of the key features of Bitcoin is that it is decentralized, meaning that it is not controlled by any government or institution. This allows for greater transparency and security in transactions, as there is no central point of failure that can be targeted by hackers.

Additionally, the use of blockchain technology, which underlies Bitcoin and other cryptocurrencies, allows for faster and cheaper transactions compared to traditional financial systems. This can greatly benefit individuals and businesses in underbanked or underdeveloped regions, as well as reducing the cost and increasing the speed of global commerce.

However, there are also concerns about the potential negative impacts of Bitcoin and other cryptocurrencies on the global financial system. These include the potential for illegal activities such as money laundering and tax evasion, as well as the volatility of the market and the lack of regulation.

Despite these concerns, it is clear that Bitcoin and other cryptocurrencies have the potential to greatly impact the future of money and the global financial system. As the technology and infrastructure surrounding these digital assets continue to mature and evolve, it will be important for governments, financial institutions, and individuals to understand and adapt to the changes brought about by this revolutionary technology.

Bonus Chapter: the best companies to buy manage and secure your bitcoins.

There are a number of companies that offer services for buying, managing, and securing bitcoins. Some of the most popular and well-established companies in the space include:

1. Coinbase: One of the most popular and user-friendly platforms for buying, selling, and storing bitcoins. It offers a mobile app and is available in over 100 countries.
2. Blockchain.com: A popular wallet provider that also offers a suite of tools for managing and trading bitcoins. It is considered one of the most secure wallet options.
3. Binance: A leading cryptocurrency exchange that offers a wide range of trading pairs, including Bitcoin.
4. Ledger: A company that offers a range of hardware wallets for storing and managing bitcoins offline, which is considered the safest way to store digital assets.
5. Trezor: Another company that offers a range of hardware wallets for storing bitcoins offline.
6. Paypal: you can set a recurring buy order for Bitcoin and ETH
7. Revolut: a fintech company that offers a range of crypto currencies
8. Nexo: a fintech regulated company that offers a range of carefully chosen crypto. Nexo offers a debit card which you can use to spend without selling your crypto.
9. Etoro: a fintech company from Israel. Although the spread is more expensive, they are a reliable company which offers a Bitcoin secured wallet and a debit card.

If you want to buy the underlying value of Bitcoin or Ethereum you can choose to invest in the following companies:

MARA
RIOT
COINBASE

MSTR (MICROSTRATEGY INC)
PAYPAL

As a rule of thumb, whatever you earn, you should always try to live with 70% of your income, put 20% in savings and 10% to pay your debts. Easier said than done but if you stick to it, you are on your way to make $1 million and more. It might be in Bitcoin only but again, a diversify portfolio is the best security you can give to yourself.

Only one thing is certain — that is, nothing is certain.

www.ingramcontent.com/pod-product-compliance
Lightning Source LLC
Chambersburg PA
CBHW050323220526
45465CB00005B/2103